LET'S VISIT
THE SOLAR SYSTEM

To the real Sebastian. I would never have written this without you. Thank you, and stay curious! **D S-M**

To my favourite Alien, Paul – beep, beep! **RL**

About the author

Dounia McMeel-Stewart first became passionate about science in high school, and has wanted to pass on that fascination and love for the subject ever since. She started writing science books for children so they could learn the exciting bits at a young age. All of her books are heavily vetted by her son, the real Sebastian, who is quick to announce when a book is boring!

For more information, please check her website: www.learningexcitement.co.uk

Let's Visit The Solar System

Text © 2020 Dounia Stewart-McMeel
Design and Illustration © Rachel Lawston, www.lawstondesign.com
Education Consultant: Paul Lawston

All rights reserved. No part of this publication may be reproduced, distributed or transmitted in any form or by any means, including photocopying, recording or other electronic or mechanical methods without written permission from the author.

ISBN: 978-1-8381516-0-7

First print edition 2020, Learning Excitement Publications
www.learningexcitement.co.uk.

LET'S VISIT
THE SOLAR SYSTEM

DOUNIA STEWART-MCMEEL
Illustrated by RACHEL LAWSTON

Howdy!

I'm an alien from a far distant galaxy. I'm on a special mission to explore your solar system. Would you like to join me?

Before we explore the wonders of your solar system, do you know what a solar system is?

Call me Sebastian.

The **solar system** is your sun, and all the planets and moons and everything else that travels around it.

It's just one part of something much, much bigger called the **Milky Way.**

The Milky Way

And the Milky Way is just one part of something even bigger called the **Universe.**

The **Universe** is the **biggest** thing there is.

The sun is at the centre of the solar system.
All the planets go around the sun.

So let's visit the **sun** first!

The scientific word for going round the sun is 'orbiting'.

Did you know that your sun is actually a **star**? All the stars you see in the night sky are actually suns. They look different from your sun as they're very far away. Isn't that amazing?

Wow, the sun is very,

very,

very,

very,

very,

very,

very,

very,

very,

VERY hot!

We'd better leave
or we'll melt!

Say hello to the planet

Mercury.

It is the closest planet to the sun, and the smallest planet in the solar system.

Moon Count: 0

Venus is upside down!

The next planet from the sun is Venus.

Hello Venus!

Even though Venus is not the closest planet to the sun, it's the hottest planet in the solar system.

Moon Count: 0

This is planet

Earth.

You live here!

Earth has one moon and humans landed there for the first time more than 50 years ago. Did you see how many moons the other planets have?

Moon Count: 1

Scientists think a LOT about whether Earth is the only planet in the solar system with people, animals and plants. Maybe one day you can help them find out!

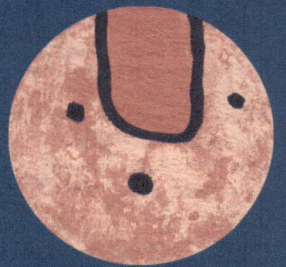

Hello planet

Mars!

Mars is called the Red Planet. Its reddish-orange colour is from the rust on its rocks.

Moon Count: 2

Oh no! There are rocks everywhere!
Watch out!!

Between Mars and Jupiter there are lots of space rocks called asteroids. This area is called the asteroid belt. It has over a million HUGE rocks.

Duck!

This striped planet is Jupiter.

Hello Jupiter!

Jupiter is the biggest planet in the solar system. It is made from gases and is so big that it is called a **gas giant**.

Moon Count: 79

Look! We're approaching Saturn and its rings.

Hello Saturn.

Saturn is a **gas giant**, just like Jupiter.

Moon Count: 82

This **ice giant** is called Uranus.

Hello Uranus!

An ice giant is a huge planet made from ice.

Moon Count: 27

Uranus travels through space on its side. It's a bit scary!

The last known planet in the solar system is Neptune.

Here it is now!

Hello Neptune!

Neptune is an **ice giant**, just like Uranus. It's the coldest planet in the solar system.

That's because it's so far from the sun.

Moon Count: 14

Neptune

This is Pluto, a dwarf planet.

Saturn

Uranus

Wow, Neptune is very,

very,

very,

very,

very,

very,

very,

very,

very,

VERY cold!

We'd better head back to planet Earth and warm up!

Jupiter

Milton Keynes UK
Ingram Content Group UK Ltd.
UKHW051928260124
436791UK00002B/13